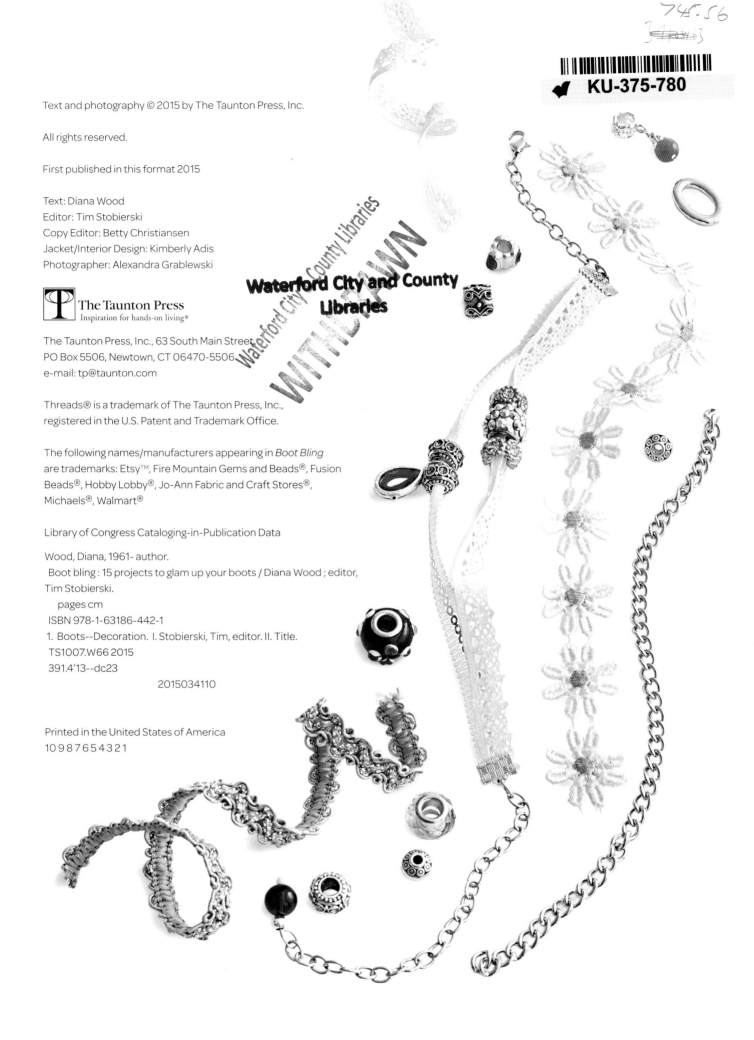

Text and photography © 2015 by The Taunton Press, Inc.

First published in this format 2015

Text: Diana Wood
Editor: Tim Stobierski
Copy Editor: Betty Christiansen
Jacket/Interior Design: Kimberly Adis
Photographer: Alexandra Grablewski

The Taunton Press
Inspiration for hands-on living®

The Taunton Press, Inc., 63 South Main Street
PO Box 5506, Newtown, CT 06470-5506
e-mail: tp@taunton.com

Threads® is a trademark of The Taunton Press, Inc.,
registered in the U.S. Patent and Trademark Office.

The following names/manufacturers appearing in *Boot Bling*
are trademarks: Etsy™, Fire Mountain Gems and Beads®, Fusion
Beads®, Hobby Lobby®, Jo-Ann Fabric and Craft Stores®,
Michaels®, Walmart®

Library of Congress Cataloging-in-Publication Data

Wood, Diana, 1961- author.
 Boot bling : 15 projects to glam up your boots / Diana Wood ; editor,
Tim Stobierski.
    pages cm
 ISBN 978-1-63186-442-1
 1. Boots--Decoration. I. Stobierski, Tim, editor. II. Title.
 TS1007.W66 2015
 391.4'13--dc23
                    2015034110

Printed in the United States of America
10 9 8 7 6 5 4 3 2 1

contents

introduction

IT SEEMS LIKE EVERYONE WEARS BOOTS OF SOME KIND!
Why not make your boots special by adding a little bling? Boot bling is jewelry that can add new life to any type of boot. It is a bracelet made with beads, ribbons, charms, and chain that you wear on the outside of your boots like an ankle bracelet. You can make it as simple or as blinged-out as you want—show your personality by adding charms and beads that reflect who you are.

You can wear boot bling on one or both boots. Try them on cowboy boots, tall boots, work boots, or winter boots. Everyone will notice and will ask you where you got your trendy and super-cool boot bling. Thanks to the great ideas and easy directions that follow, you'll be able to tell them you made it yourself.

what you'll need

CRIMPING TOOLS
Many of the projects in this booklet require pliers to twist jewelry wire or open jump rings. I used crimp-style pliers and round-nose pliers, but you can also use any kind of pliers that can grip on to a jump ring.

WIRE CUTTER
A standard jewelry wire cutter can be used to cut wire or jewelry pins when making dangles.

SCISSORS
You'll need scissors to cut the ribbon to the right length.

EYE PINS
You'll use eye pins to create your own dangles. These pins act as the backbone on which you'll build your dangles.

RIBBON CLAMPS
These clamps are used to keep your layers of ribbon and chain connected and in order. They come in a variety of sizes.

GLUE
You will need a strong glue for many of the projects in this booklet. You can use any glue of your choice, but I use E6000 fabric glue. Whatever glue you use, be sure to follow the manufacturer's directions for drying and setting. I let my glue set for a minimum of 30 minutes.

EMBELLISHMENTS
Many of these projects feature bead dangles that are easily made by hand (see p. 7 for instructions on making your own dangle). You can also use a variety of rhinestones, beads, charms, found items—virtually anything—to adorn your boot bling. Get creative with your chains and ribbons for some added interest! You will need to use beads with a hole large enough to get a ribbon through.

You will want to use chains with smaller links that you can also thread through a wide-hole bead. You might also raid your mother's costume jewelry for special finds or go to the local thrift store.

RIBBONS AND FABRIC FLOWERS
You can use any kind of ribbon or fabric flowers, though it is best to use ribbon less than 1 in. in width, and you don't want it to be too stiff. The best selection of ribbon and fabric flowers I've found is in the scrapbooking section of my local craft store.

techniques

You only need to master a few easy techniques in order to start making your very own boot bling. The text and photos that follow will guide you through all of the processes that I use in my projects. Once you've mastered these techniques, have fun and experiment in making your own bead dangles and boot bling!

GLUING A CHAIN TO RIBBON

Line up one end of the ribbon with one end of the chain. Cover the chain and fabric at one end with a good-sized dollop of glue. Let this set for 30 minutes.

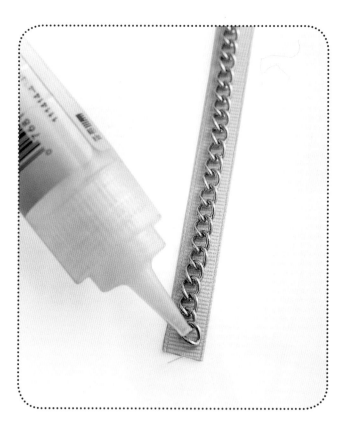

ATTACHING A CRIMP

1. Line up the end of the ribbon into the ribbon crimp.

2. Using crimp-style pliers, gently squeeze the pliers onto the ribbon crimp and firmly crimp it. I crimp in the middle and on each side of the ribbon crimp.

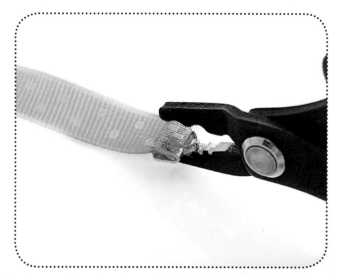

MAKING A BEAD DANGLE

To make a bead dangle that will hang on the back of the boot:

1. Obtain 3 to 4 small- to medium-sized beads. These beads need to have a small opening.

2. Thread the beads onto a beading pin. If the hole in the bead is too large, they will fall off the pin. You can also use a regular straight pin that you use with fabric.

3. Once you have all of the beads on the pin, bend the pin above the last bead at a 90-degree angle.

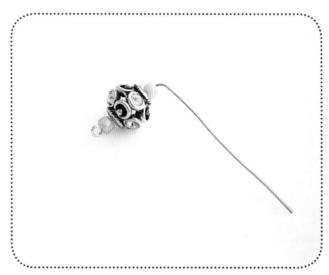

4. The remaining portion of the pin now needs to be trimmed. Cut the pin so that there is 1 in. of pin remaining—enough to make a loop.

5. With round-nose pliers, grab the end of the pin and wrap it around the pliers. Use the middle portion of the pliers to shape your loop, as shown.

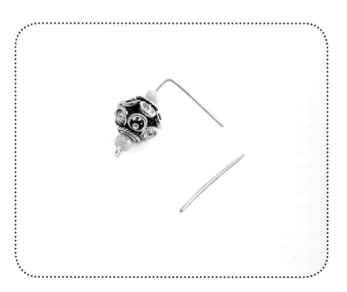

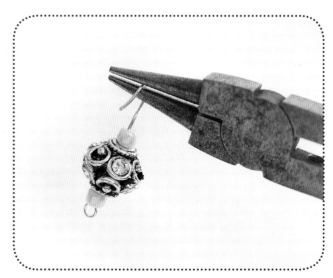

CUTTING RIBBON AT 45 DEGREES

If you are using 1 in. or wider ribbon, you may find it easier to cut both ends of the ribbon at a 45-degree angle. The photo below shows the right side of the ribbon. On the left side, cut it in the opposite direction so that when you are done, the top of the ribbon is shorter than the bottom. This 45-degree cut allows you to add a ribbon crimp at an angle so that the boot bling hangs better on your boot.

ADDING A LOBSTER CLASP

To finish off your boot bling with a lobster clasp, you can either use pliers to open the last chain link, or you can add a jump ring to the last chain link. Open the jump ring/chain link and slide the clasp on, then close the jump ring/chain link with the pliers.

ADDING YOUR BEAD DANGLE TO A CHAIN

There's no point in making a bead dangle if you can't add it to your boot bling! Using a pair of needle-nose pliers, slightly pry open the loop that you created to finish your bead dangle. Thread the loop into the final link in the chain, and close the loop securely.

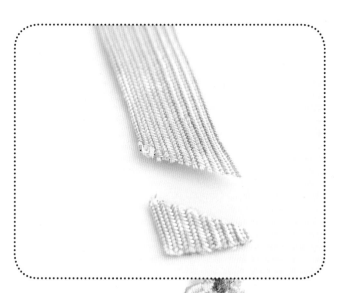

night on the town

Night on the Town is a beautiful boot bling for everyday wear. This is a very easy boot bling using ribbons and some chain. Use any colors for the hanging charm—your school colors, your favorite sports team's colors—anything goes.

WHAT YOU NEED

7 in. of ½-in.-wide white lace ribbon

7 in. of ½-in.-wide white ribbon with sparkle

Two ½-in. ribbon crimps

5 ring beads

1 hanging charm

6 in. of chain (cut into 2-in. and 4-in. pieces)

Lobster clasp

Crimping tool

1 bead dangle (optional)

1. Stack the ribbons on top of each other, making sure the ends match up. You can decide which ribbon will sit on top. Position the right side of the ribbons into the ribbon crimp. Using a crimping tool, crimp the ribbons in place (see p. 6 for instructions on crimping ribbon).

2. On the top ribbon, add 3 beads. It is important to select beads that can accommodate the thickness of the ribbon. On the bottom ribbon, add the remaining 2 beads and the hanging charm (1 bead should sit on each side of the charm for a symmetrical look). When you are happy with your bead placement, position the left side of the ribbons into the remaining ribbon crimp, and crimp in place.

3. Using a crimping tool, open the last link on the 2-in. piece of chain and connect it to the right ribbon crimp. Open the chain link on the other end of the 2-in. piece of chain and connect the lobster clasp (see p. 8 for instructions on adding a lobster clasp to a length of chain). Open a chain link on the 4-in. length of chain and attach it to the left ribbon crimp. If desired, add a bead dangle to the other end of the 4-in. length of chain (see p. 7 for instructions on making a bead dangle).

tip Measure the circumference of your boot before making your boot bling to make sure it will fit. You want the bling to fit all the way around your ankle. It should be loose enough that it dangles slightly, but tight enough that it does not fall down. Adjust your lengths of ribbon and chain to suit your boot.

baby blue

Simple yet eye-catching, this boot bling will capture the attention of everyone on a beautiful, clear blue-sky day. This bling pairs beautifully with lighter-colored boots.

WHAT YOU NEED

7 in. of ¼-in.-wide silver ribbon with sparkle

7 in. of ½-in.-wide white lace ribbon

7 in. of ½-in.-wide blue ribbon

7 in. of thin light blue rope ribbon

Two ½-in. ribbon crimps

3 ring beads

2 blue glass beads

1 hanging charm

7 in. of chain (cut into 3-in. and 4-in. pieces)

Lobster clasp

Crimping tool

Strong glue of your choice

1 bead dangle (optional)

1. Glue the ¼-in. silver ribbon onto the front of the white lace ribbon and let set for 30 minutes or until dry. Lay the white lace ribbon on your work surface with the silver side up. Then stack the white ribbon on top of the blue ribbon and the blue rope ribbon, with the rope ribbon centered on the bottom. Make sure the ends match. Position the right side of the ribbons into the ribbon crimp. Using a crimping tool, crimp the ribbons in place (see p. 6 for instructions on crimping ribbon).

2. Thread the beads onto the blue ribbon. I used 3 ring beads with sparkle and 2 blue glass beads, alternating them to create my design. Thread the hanging charm onto the rope ribbon. When you are happy with the bead placement, position the left side of the ribbons into the remaining ribbon crimp, and crimp in place.

3. Using a crimping tool, open the last link on the 3-in. length of chain and connect it to the left ribbon crimp. Open the chain link on the other end of the 3-in. piece of chain and connect the lobster clasp (see p. 8 for instructions on adding a lobster clasp to a length of chain). Open a chain link on the 4-in. length of chain and attach it to the right ribbon crimp. If desired, add a bead dangle to the other end of the 4-in. length of chain (see p. 7 for instructions on making a bead dangle).

tip If you want just a hint of silver in your design, glue the silver ribbon to the back of the white lace ribbon instead of the front. The silver ribbon will then only show through the holes in the lace, for a more subdued look.

mermaid drop

This turquoise ribbon boot bling will make any mermaid sing! Combining simple colors with a large statement bead, this bling is perfect for anyone trying to make a fashion splash.

WHAT YOU NEED

11 in. of ½-in.-wide transparent patterned turquoise ribbon

11 in. of ¼-in.-wide silver ribbon

11 in. of ⅛-in.-wide plain turquoise ribbon

One ½-in. ribbon crimp package (this will come with one crimp with a lobster clasp and another crimp with chain attached)

4 turquoise glass beads

2 ring beads

1 hanging charm

1 fabric flower

Crimping tool

Strong glue of your choice

1. Stack the ribbons on top of each other with the transparent ribbon on the bottom, followed by the silver ribbon in the middle and the smaller turquoise ribbon on top. Make sure the ends match. Position the right side of the ribbons into the ribbon crimp. Using a crimping tool s, crimp the ribbons in place (see p. 6 for instructions on crimping ribbon).

2. Begin adding the beads. You will thread the beads onto all 3 lengths of ribbon. Start with 3 beads with large holes, then add the hanging charm, followed by the remaining beads. I used a combination of glass beads and ring beads for mine, positioning them so they appear even on both sides of the hanging charm. When you are happy with your bead placement, position the left side of the ribbons into the remaining ribbon crimp, and crimp in place.

3. Glue the fabric flower where you want it and let it set for 30 minutes, or until dry.

tip Glass beads add some interest and texture to your bling. If you want something a little more cohesive, opt for beads in one color.

rock star

Nothing says rock'n'roll quite like this bold bling. Rock your boots and dance up a storm with this perfect complement to your outfit.

WHAT YOU NEED

20 in. of ¼-in.-wide silver ribbon with sparkle

20 in. of ½-in.-wide silver ribbon with sparkle

1 charm with holes on each side that you can fit the ribbon through

1 fabric flower

Two ½-in. ribbon crimps

4 in. of chain (cut into 1-in. and 3-in. pieces)

Lobster clasp

Crimping tool

Strong glue of your choice

1 bead dangle (optional)

1. Cut each 20-in. length of ribbon in half so that you have two 10-in. lengths of each ribbon. Take one 10-in. length of the ¼-in. ribbon and stack it on top of one 10-in. length of the ½-in. ribbon. Thread this ribbon through the right side of the charm and bring it back so that all 4 ends of ribbon line up. Position the ribbon ends into the ribbon crimp. Using a crimping tool, crimp the ribbon ends in place (see p. 6 for instructions on crimping ribbon). Repeat this process for the left side of the charm, using the remaining ribbon.

2. Using a crimping tool, open the last link on the 1-in. piece of chain and connect it to the right ribbon crimp. Open the chain link on the other end of the 1-in. piece of chain and connect the lobster clasp (see p. 8 for instructions on adding a lobster clasp to a length of chain). Open a chain link on the 3-in. length of chain and attach it to the left ribbon crimp. If desired, add a bead dangle to the other end of the 3-in. length of chain (see p. 7 for instructions on making a bead dangle).

3. Glue the fabric flower where you want it and let it set for 30 minutes, or until dry.

tip As long as the holes on your charm are large enough, you can use as many different types of ribbon as you want. Instead of two types, why not try four different kinds of sparkly ribbon?

13

touch of silver

Talk about over the top! This sparkly ribbon and charm bling adds a ton of character to any outfit. A delicate flower counterbalances the hanging charm for a truly pulled-together look.

WHAT YOU NEED

9 in. of ½-in.-wide gray ribbon with sparkle

9 in. of ½-in.-wide patterned gray ribbon

Two ½-in. ribbon crimps

1 hanging charm

4 ring beads (2 with thick bands and 2 with thin bands)

5 in. of chain (cut into 2-in. and 3-in. pieces)

1 fabric flower

Lobster clasp

Crimping tool

Strong glue of your choice

1 bead dangle (optional)

tip Craft stores carry a wide variety of ribbon in a range of designs. Really add interest to your bling by choosing the perfect ribbons for your style.

1. Stack the sparkly ribbon on top of the patterned gray ribbon, making sure the ends match. Position the right side of the ribbons into the ribbon crimp. Using a crimping tool, crimp the ribbons in place (see p. 6 for instructions on crimping ribbon).

2. Thread the beads onto the patterned gray ribbon. I used a variety of ring beads and placed 2 beads on either side of my hanging charm. When you are happy with your bead placement, position the left side of the ribbons into the remaining ribbon crimp, and crimp in place.

3. Using a crimping tool, open the last link on the 2-in. piece of chain and connect it to the right ribbon crimp. Open the chain link on the other end of the 2-in. piece of chain and connect the lobster clasp (see p. 8 for instructions on adding a lobster clasp to a length of chain). Open a chain link on the 3-in. length of chain and attach it to the left ribbon crimp. If desired, add a bead dangle to the other end of the 3-in. length of chain (see p. 7 for instructions on making a bead dangle).

4. Glue the fabric flower where you want it and let it set for 30 minutes, or until dry.

lacy dreams

Be bold—bring on the flower power with this pink flower and love charm boot bling. You can wear this boot bling in several different ways: Position the flower on the top or the side of your boot.

WHAT YOU NEED

24 in. of ½-in.-wide white rope ribbon

One ½-in. ribbon crimp package (this will come with 1 crimp with a lobster clasp and another crimp with chain attached)

1 closed ring charm

1 hanging charm

3 fabric flowers

Crimping tool

Strong glue of your choice

1. Divide the 24 in. of ribbon into 2 even pieces (each will measure 12 in.). This type of ribbon tends to fray when cut. To prevent this, add a dab of glue to each end and allow it to set for 30 minutes, or until dry.

2. Thread 1 of the 12-in. lengths of ribbon through the right side of the ring charm and bring it back so that both ends line up. Position the ribbon ends into the ribbon crimp. Using a crimping tool, crimp the ribbon ends in place (see p. 6 for instructions on crimping ribbon). Repeat this process for the left side of the charm, using the remaining ribbon.

3. Attach the hanging charm directly to the ring charm using a crimping tool. Glue the fabric flowers where you want them and let them set for 30 minutes, or until dry. I used 1 large pink flower and 2 smaller white flowers for variety.

tip When designing your boot bling, try to keep your design balanced for a stylish look. For this project, I placed the large pink flower on one side of the charm and the two small white flowers on the other side of the charm for balance.

black tie affair

A combination of silver and black makes this bling perfect for an elegant outing or event. Whether at a wedding, a holiday party, or a night out with the girls, this bling will show off your originality and class.

WHAT YOU NEED

**9 in. of ¼-in.- or ½-in.-wide
    black ribbon with sparkle**
**15 in. of small link chain
    (cut into an 11-in. piece and
    two 2-in. pieces)**
1 hanging charm
**3 fabric flowers, 1 black and
    2 white**
Two ½-in. ribbon crimps
Lobster clasp
Crimping tool
Strong glue of your choice

1. Lay the 11-in. length of chain on top of the black ribbon. Glue the right end of the chain to the right end of the ribbon and let set for 30 minutes, or until dry (see p. 6 for instructions on gluing chain to ribbon). This will help keep the chain from shifting around while you work. Position the right side of the ribbon/chain into the ribbon crimp. Using a crimping tool, crimp the right side in place (see p. 6 for instructions on crimping ribbon).

2. Thread the hanging charm onto the length of chain. Glue the left end of the chain to the left end of the ribbon and let set for 30 minutes, or until dry. Position the left side of the ribbon/chain into the ribbon crimp, and crimp in place.

3. Using a crimping tool, open the last link on one 2-in. piece of chain and connect it to the right ribbon crimp. Open the chain link on the other end of the 2-in. piece of chain

and connect the lobster clasp (see p. 8 for instructions on adding a lobster clasp to a length of chain). Open a chain link on the remaining 2-in. length of chain and attach it to the left ribbon crimp.

4. Glue the fabric flowers onto the ribbon where you want them and let them set for 30 minutes, or until dry. I placed a black fabric flower in the center of the black ribbon and then placed a white fabric flower on either side.

turquoise petals

This bling is boho chic at its best. A large turquoise flower paired with beads in complementary shades of blue work together to bring this bling to life.

WHAT YOU NEED

- 10 in. of ½-in.-wide transparent turquoise ribbon
- 10 in. of ½-in.-wide turquoise ribbon with sparkle
- Two ½-in. ribbon crimps
- 1 hanging charm
- 3 ring beads
- 1 large fabric flower
- 5 in. of chain (cut into 2-in. and 3-in. pieces)
- Lobster clasp
- Crimping tool
- Strong glue of your choice
- 1 bead dangle (optional)

1. Lay the transparent turquoise ribbon on top of the sparkly turquoise ribbon, making sure the ends match. Using a crimping tool, crimp the right side of the ribbons in place (see p. 6 for instructions on crimping ribbon).

2. Thread the beads onto the transparent turquoise ribbon. The beads you use and their placement is completely up to you—I used a variety of ring beads. I placed 2 ring beads on the ribbon, followed by a hanging charm and the remaining ring bead. When you are happy with your bead placement, position the left side of the ribbons into the remaining ribbon crimp, and crimp in place.

3. Using a crimping tool, open the last link on the 2-in. piece of chain and connect it to the right ribbon crimp. Open the chain link on the other end of the 2-in. piece of chain and connect the lobster clasp (see p. 8 for instructions on adding a lobster clasp to a length of chain). Open a chain link on the 3-in. length of chain and attach it to the left ribbon crimp. If desired, add a bead dangle to the other end of the 3-in. length of chain (see p. 7 for instructions on making a bead dangle).

4. Glue the fabric flower where you want it and let it set for 30 minutes, or until dry.

> **tip** If desired, you can replace the fabric flower with any of a number of other embellishments. Try a feather, button, or lightweight charm.

silver & pearls

Make some noise with this sparkly bling and beautiful silver ribbons. The light color of the ribbon and beads will work with any boot and will make it a standout.

WHAT YOU NEED

9 in. of ½-in.-wide patterned gray flat ribbon

9 in. of silver rope ribbon

9 in. of ½-in.-wide white ribbon with sparkle

Two ½-in. ribbon crimps

4 ring beads (2 silver and 2 pearl)

1 hanging charm

5 in. of chain (cut into 3-in. and 2-in. pieces)

Crimping tool

Lobster clasp

1 bead dangle (optional)

1. Stack the ribbons so the patterned gray ribbon is on the bottom, followed by the silver rope ribbon in the middle and the white ribbon on top. Stagger the placement in the crimp so that it suits you. Position the right side of the ribbon into the ribbon crimp. Using a crimping tool, crimp the right side in place (see p. 6 for instructions on crimping ribbon).

2. Thread the beads onto the silver ribbon and the silver rope ribbon. *Do not thread the beads onto the white ribbon.* I used 2 silver ring beads and 2 pearl ring beads. I placed one of each on the ribbons, followed by my hanging charm, followed by the remaining 2 beads. When you are happy with your bead placement, position the left side of the ribbons into the remaining ribbon crimp, and crimp in place.

3. Using a crimping tool, open the last link on the 2-in. piece of chain and connect it to the right ribbon crimp. Open the chain link on the other end of the 2-in. piece of chain and connect the lobster clasp (see p. 8 for instructions on adding a lobster clasp to a length of chain). Open a chain link on the 3-in. length of chain and attach it to the left ribbon crimp. If desired, add a bead dangle to the other end of the 3-in. length of chain (see p. 7 for instructions on making a bead dangle).

tip When placing your hanging charm, make sure it is facing the correct way! You don't want to finish your boot bling only to discover that the central bead is facing your boot—it should be facing the world!

flower power

Channel your inner hippie with this super-cute bling featuring flowers and colorful beads. Pair with moccasins for a perfect flower child outing.

WHAT YOU NEED

8 in. of small silver rope ribbon

7 in. of flower-style ribbon

6 ring beads

2 small hanging charms

1 large hanging charm

6 in. of chain (cut into two 3-in. pieces)

Crimping tool

Lobster clasp

1. Arrange the ribbon so that the silver rope ribbon sits on top of the flower-style ribbon. Make sure the ends match. Position the right side of the ribbons into the ribbon crimp. Using a crimping tool, crimp the ribbons in place (see p. 6 for instructions on crimping ribbon).

2. Thread the beads onto the silver rope ribbon in the following order: 1 ring bead, 1 small hanging charm, 2 ring beads, 1 large hanging charm, 2 ring beads, 1 small hanging charm, 1 ring bead. When you are happy with your bead placement, position the left side of the ribbons into the remaining ribbon crimp, and crimp in place.

3. Using a crimping tool, open the last link on one 3-in. piece of chain and connect it to the right ribbon crimp. Open the chain link on the other end of the 3-in. piece of chain and connect the lobster clasp (see p. 8 for instructions on adding a lobster clasp to a length of chain). Open a chain link on the remaining 3-in. length of chain and attach it to the left ribbon crimp.

lucky for you

Bring good luck with you wherever you go by attaching your lucky charm to your bling. I chose a lucky horseshoe, but you can go with any charm that suits you—try a four-leaf clover or a wishbone.

WHAT YOU NEED

9 in. of ¼-in.-wide silver ribbon with sparkle

9 in. of ½-in.-wide patterned pink ribbon

9 in. of ½-in.-wide plain pink ribbon

Two 1-in. ribbon crimps

6 in. of chain (cut into two 3-in. pieces)

4 ring beads

1 hanging charm

2 pink fabric flowers

Crimping tool

Lobster clasp

Strong glue of your choice

1 bead dangle (optional)

1. Glue the ¼-in. silver ribbon onto the front of the patterned pink ribbon and let set for 30 minutes, or until dry. Arrange your ribbon so that the plain pink ribbon is on top of the patterned pink ribbon, but staggered in the crimp so that the silver ribbon is visible. Make sure the ends match. Position the right side of the ribbons into the ribbon crimp. Using a crimping tool, crimp the ribbons in place (see p. 6 for instructions on crimping ribbon).

NOTE: *When using a 1-in. ribbon crimp, the ribbons will lie better if you cut the ends at 45 degrees. See p. 8 for instructions on cutting ribbon at 45 degrees.*

2. Thread the beads and hanging charm onto the plain pink ribbon. I used 2 pearl-style ring beads and 2 ring beads with sparkle, placing one of each on either side of my hanging charm. When you are happy with your bead placement, position the left side of the ribbons into the remaining ribbon crimp, and crimp in place.

3. Using a crimping tool, open the last link on one 3-in. piece of chain and connect it to the right ribbon crimp. Open the chain link on the other end of the 3-in. piece of chain and connect the lobster clasp (see p. 8 for instructions on adding a lobster clasp to a length of chain). Open a chain link on the remaining 3-in. length of chain and attach it to the left ribbon crimp. If desired, add a bead dangle to the other end of the 3-in. length of chain (see p. 7 for instructions on making a bead dangle).

> **tip** Why settle for just one lucky charm? Load up this bling with as many good luck symbols as you can think up. Green ribbon instead of pink can work well with a four-leaf clover theme.

girly girl polka dots

Cute and delicate, this pink boot bling is the perfect addition to any boot. The love charm will have your friends love, love, loving it. You can keep it simple, or add more ribbons and beads for a more intricate look.

WHAT YOU NEED

8 in. of ½-in.-wide patterned pink ribbon

8 in. of small silver rope ribbon

8 in. of ¼-in.-wide white ribbon with sparkle

Two ½-in. ribbon crimps

7 in. of chain (cut into 4-in. and 3-in. pieces)

2 ring beads

1 hanging charm

Crimping tool

Lobster clasp

1 bead dangle (optional)

1. Lay the ribbons out so that the patterned pink ribbon is on the bottom, followed by the silver rope ribbon in the middle and the white ribbon on top. Position the right side of the ribbon into the ribbon crimp. Using a crimping tool, crimp the right side in place (see p. 6 for instructions on crimping ribbon).

2. Thread the hanging charm onto the patterned pink ribbon and the silver rope ribbon. *Do not thread the hanging charm onto the white ribbon.* Then thread the 2 remaining beads onto the white ribbon only. When you are happy with the bead placement, position the left side of the ribbons into the remaining ribbon crimp, and crimp in place.

3. Using a crimping tool, open the last link on the 3-in. piece of chain and connect it to the right ribbon crimp. Open the chain link on the other end of the 3-in. piece of chain and connect the lobster clasp (see p. 8 for instructions on adding a lobster clasp to a length of chain). Open a chain link on the 4-in. length of chain and attach it to the left ribbon crimp. If desired, add a bead dangle to the other end of the 4-in. length of chain (see p. 7 for instructions on making a bead dangle).

> **tip** Go bold with your bead dangles. Why not make two or three and attach them to your bling for some added oomph?

pom-pom perfect

Who can resist pom-poms? This bling combines all of the best things about being crafty—ribbon, beads, and adorable white pom-poms. Up the cuteness by using colored pom-poms, or dye the white ones any color you want.

WHAT YOU NEED

7 in. of small hot pink rope ribbon

7 in. of white ribbon with pom-poms

8 in. of ½-in.-wide silver ribbon

6 ring beads

1 hanging charm

Two ½-in. ribbon crimps

8 in. of chain (cut into two 4-in. pieces)

Crimping tool

Lobster clasp

Strong glue of your choice

1 bead dangle (optional)

1. Glue the hot pink rope ribbon onto the front of the white ribbon with pom-poms and let set for 30 minutes, or until dry. Arrange your ribbons so that the silver ribbon is on the bottom and the white ribbon with pom-poms is on top. Stagger in the crimp as necessary. Position the right side of the ribbon into the ribbon crimp. Using a crimping tool, crimp the right side in place (see p. 6 for instructions on crimping ribbon).

2. Thread the beads and hanging charm onto the silver ribbon only. I used a variety of sparkly ring beads, pearl-style ring beads, and gemstone ring beads. I placed one of each type of ring bead onto the ribbon, followed by the hanging charm, then followed by the remaining ring beads. When you are happy with the bead placement, position the left side of the ribbons into the remaining ribbon crimp, and crimp in place.

3. Using a crimping tool, open the last link on one 4-in. length of chain and connect it to the right ribbon crimp. Open the chain link on the other end of the 4-in. piece of chain and connect the lobster clasp (see p. 8 for instructions on adding a lobster clasp to a length of chain).

tip If the pom-poms are too much for you, you can just use any plain white or lace ribbon.

Open a chain link on the remaining 4-in. length of chain and attach it to the left ribbon crimp. If desired, add a bead dangle to the other end of the 4-in. length of chain (see p. 7 for instructions on making a bead dangle).

orange blossom fairy garden

A fairy charm coupled with a variety of flowers will make everyone think there's something magical about this special bling.

WHAT YOU NEED

8 in. of ¼-in.-wide silver ribbon
    with sparkle
8 in. of ½-in.-wide plain
    orange ribbon
8 in. of ½-in.-wide patterned
    orange ribbon
9 in. of white rope ribbon
Two ½-in. ribbon crimps
2 ring beads
1 hanging charm
3 fabric flowers, 1 orange and 2 white
6 in. of chain (cut into two 3-in. pieces)
Crimping tool
Lobster clasp
Strong glue of your choice
1 bead dangle (optional)

1. Glue the ¼-in. silver ribbon onto the front of the plain orange ribbon and let set for 30 minutes, or until dry. Stack the ribbons so that the patterned orange ribbon is on the bottom, followed by the plain orange ribbon in the middle and the white rope ribbon on top. Stagger the ribbons in the crimp to suit you, but make sure the white rope ribbon is slightly lower than the others so that it can dangle. Position the right side of the ribbon into the ribbon crimp. Using a crimping tool, crimp the right side in place (see p. 6 for instructions on crimping ribbon).

2. Thread 1 ring bead onto the open end of the white rope ribbon, followed by the hanging charm, then followed by the remaining ring bead. When you are happy with your bead placement, position the left side of the ribbons into the remaining ribbon crimp, and crimp in place.

3. Using a crimping tool, open the last link on one 3-in. piece of chain and connect it to the right ribbon crimp. Open the chain link on the other end of the chain and connect the lobster clasp (see p. 8 for instructions on adding a lobster clasp to a length of chain). Open a chain link on the remaining 3-in. length of chain and attach it to the left ribbon crimp. If desired, add a bead dangle to the other end of the 4-in. length of chain (see p. 7 for instructions on making a bead dangle).

4. Glue the fabric flowers where you want them and let them set for 30 minutes, or until dry.

tip If you finish making your boot bling and realize that you made a mistake along the way, you may be able to salvage the project. Very carefully, pry one ribbon clamp open with pliers. Make your changes and reclamp the project together.

giddy-up cowgirl

You don't need to go for a long ride to love this easy-to-make boot bling. Combining the chain with the ribbon gives this bling some added depth and interest.

WHAT YOU NEED

9 in. of ¼-in.-wide silver ribbon with sparkle

9 in. of ½-in.-wide silver ribbon with sparkle

Two 1-in. ribbon crimps

16 inches of chain (cut into two 3-in. pieces and one 10-in. piece)

2 ring beads

3 hanging charms

Crimping tool

Lobster clasp

Strong glue of your choice

tip This boot bling pairs nicely with your favorite cowboy boots. Tone down the cowboy look by using turquoise charms instead of the hanging charms.

1. Arrange the ribbons so that the ¼-in. silver ribbon sits under the ½-in. silver ribbon. The 10-in. length of chain should also sit under the ½-in. silver ribbon. Stagger the ribbons so that the chain sits lower than the ¼-in. silver ribbon. Make sure the ends match. Glue the right end of the chain to the right end of the ½-in. ribbon and let set for 30 minutes, or until dry (see p. 6 for instructions on gluing chain to ribbon). This will help keep the chain from shifting around while you work. Position the right side of the ribbon/chain into the ribbon crimp. Using a crimping tool, crimp the right side in place (see p. 6 for instructions on crimping ribbon).

NOTE: *When using a 1-in. ribbon clamp, the ribbons will lie better if you cut the ends at 45 degrees. See p. 8 for instructions on cutting ribbon at 45 degrees.*

2. Flip the chain over the top of the ½-in. ribbon so that it drapes, as shown. Thread the hanging charms and beads onto the ¼-in. silver ribbon, which will hang between the ½-in. ribbon and the chain. I alternated mine so that a ring bead sits between each of my hanging charms. Glue the left end of the chain to the left end of the ribbon and let set for 30 minutes, or until dry. Position the left side of the ribbon/chain into the ribbon crimp, and crimp in place.

3. Using a crimping tool, open the last link on one 3-in. length of chain and connect it to the right ribbon crimp. Open the chain link on the other end of the 3-in. piece of chain and connect the lobster clasp (see p. 8 for instructions on adding a lobster clasp to a length of chain). Open a chain link on the remaining 3-in. length of chain and attach it to the left ribbon crimp.

resources

Local jewelry and bead shops can yield some remarkable finds. If you can't find a local store, these craft store chains and online retailers offer excellent supplies for making these projects.

A BEAD STORE
www.abeadstore.com

Jewelry-making supplies, beads, charms, and chain

A.C. MOORE
www.acmoore.com

Fabric and craft supplies

ETSY™
www.etsy.com

Unique and vintage beads, charms, fabrics, ribbons, and many craft supplies

FIRE MOUNTAIN GEMS AND BEADS®
www.firemountaingems. com

Jewelry-making supplies, beads, and charms

FUSION BEADS®
www.fusionbeads.com

Jewelry-making supplies, beads, charms, and chain

HOBBY LOBBY®
www.hobbylobby.com

Jewelry-making supplies, beads, charms, and many other craft supplies

JO-ANN FABRIC AND CRAFT STORES®
www.joann.com

Jewelry-making supplies, beads, charms, ribbon, lace, fabrics, and many other craft supplies

MICHAELS®
www.michaels.com

Jewelry-making supplies, beads, charms, and many other craft supplies

WALMART®
www.walmart.com

Craft and art supplies

metric equivalents

One inch equals approximately 2.54 centimeters. To convert inches to centimeters, multiply the figure in inches by 2.54 and round off to the nearest half centimeter, or use the chart below, whose figures are rounded off (1 centimeter equals 10 millimeters).

⅛ in. = 3 mm	9 in. = 23 cm
¼ in. = 6 mm	10 in. = 25.5 cm
⅜ in. = 1 cm	12 in. = 30.5 cm
½ in. = 1.3 cm	14 in. = 35.5 cm
⅝ in. = 1.5 cm	15 in. = 38 cm
¾ in. = 2 cm	16 in. = 40.5 cm
⅞ in. = 2.2 cm	18 in. = 45.5 cm
1 in. = 2.5 cm	20 in. = 51 cm
2 in. = 5 cm	21 in. = 53.5 cm
3 in. = 7.5 cm	22 in. = 56 cm
4 in. = 10 cm	24 in. = 61 cm
5 in. = 12.5 cm	25 in. = 63.5 cm
6 in. = 15 cm	36 in. = 92 cm
7 in. = 18 cm	45 in. = 114.5 cm
8 in. = 20.5 cm	60 in. = 152 cm

If you like these projects, you'll love these other fun craft booklets

Arm Knitting
Linda Zemba Burhance
EAN: 9781627108867
8$\frac{1}{2}$ × 10$\frac{7}{8}$, 32 pages
Product #078045, $9.95 U.S.

Fashionista Arm Knitting
Linda Zemba Burhance
EAN: 9781627109567
8$\frac{1}{2}$ × 10$\frac{7}{8}$, 32 pages
Product # 078050, $9.95 U.S.

Bungee Band Bracelets & More
Vera Vandenbosch
EAN: 9781627108898
8$\frac{1}{2}$ × 10$\frac{7}{8}$, 32 pages
Product # 078048, $9.95 U.S.

Mini Macramé
Vera Vandenbosch
EAN: 9781627109574
8$\frac{1}{2}$ × 10$\frac{7}{8}$, 32 pages
Product # 078049, $9.95 U.S.

DecoDen Bling
Alice Fisher
EAN: 9781627108874
8$\frac{1}{2}$ × 10$\frac{7}{8}$, 32 pages
Product # 078046, $9.95 U.S.

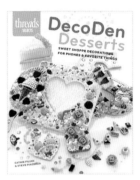

DecoDen Desserts
Cathie Filian and Steve Piacenza
EAN: 9781627109703
8$\frac{1}{2}$ × 10$\frac{7}{8}$, 32 pages
Product # 078053, $9.95 U.S.

Super Cute Duct Tape
Jayna Maleri
EAN: 9781627109901
8$\frac{1}{2}$ × 10$\frac{7}{8}$, 32 page
Product # 078056, $9.95 U.S.

Rubber Band Charm Jewelry
Maggie Marron
EAN: 9781627108881
8$\frac{1}{2}$ × 10$\frac{7}{8}$, 32 page
Product # 078047, $9.95 U.S.

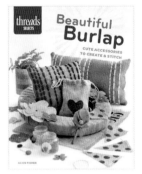

Beautiful Burlap
Alice Fisher
EAN: 9781627109888
8$\frac{1}{2}$ × 10$\frac{7}{8}$, 32 page
Product # 078054, $9.95 U.S.

Shop for these and other great craft books and booklets online: www.tauntonstore.com

Simply search by product number or call 800-888-8286, use code MX800126
Call Monday-Friday 9AM – 9PM EST and Saturday 9AM – 5PM EST.
International customers, call 203-702-2204